Sodium

Carole Bromley

Calder Valley
Poetry

Published 2019 by Calder Valley Poetry
www.caldervalleypoetry.com
caldervalleypoetry@yahoo.com

ISBN 978-1-9160387-4-5

Designed and typeset in Garamond by Bob Horne

Printed by Amadeus Press, Ezra House, West 26 Business Park,
Cleckheaton, West Yorkshire, BD19 4TQ.
www.amadeuspress.co.uk

Contents

for John

Benign Cyst Pressing on Optic Nerve

The old lady opposite doesn't know
what day it is. I tell her Sunday
though I'm losing track myself.

All night she laboured back and
forth to the toilet
and didn't close the door,

it took four of them to get her
into bed. Liz has lost
the use of both of her legs.

Sharon says the doctor told her
she was going nutty.
She's missing her dogs

and has photos of them
on a pillow under her head.
She thinks she will lose her kids.

Jean lay for thirty hours on her floor.
She tells me with pride: *I managed
to only wet myself three times.*

Today I'm not crying. I'm resigned
to the drip and the long wait
to be transferred to Hull

where I will meet
the man who will drill
inside my skull.

Reading Henry James in Hospital

What Maisie Knew. I haven't read it
for fifty years. I knew nothing then,
only the rhythm of his prose,
that Maisie was the centre of consciousness,
that I would need to sit up late
to finish it before the tutorial,
swigging from a tooth mug
the port I stole from formal dinner.
For me the book will always taste
of peppermint and port and the summer of love.

I turn the pages with my cannula'd hand,
wander away from Sharon glued to *Corrie*,
from Jean flipping through *Take a Break,*
from Joan's painful voyage to the toilet.
'I say, I say, do look out', Sir Claude
quite amiably protested. Sister trips
over the zimmer Jean parked by my bed,
tells me not to keep my frame there.
I do not have a frame, I protest.
Jean looks up from her article. *Yet.*

Ambulance Ride

My Poetry Society bag is on my lap,
Take if you must this little bag of dreams;
the drip hung from a hook. A jolt
as the gurney hits the hoist, that blast of air.
We'll soon get you warmed up. They ask me
which route I would take. The driver says
he thinks he'll put the flasher on but not the siren.
After three minutes the siren goes on too.
I can't be doing with traffic jams!
I watch as we go through every red light.
The ambulance man gives me a sick bowl,
apologises for the bumpiness of the ride,
holds the gurney steady with his foot,
fills in a pink form, gives me a pain killer,
tells me about his earlier calls, the RTA,
the one-year-old he drew a face on a glove for,
says he and his wife wanted kids but it never happened.
When we arrive on the ward I feel lost.
A man walks up and down like a zombie,
his spine and head held up in a cage.
In my bay two women with bandaged scalps
vomit in cardboard bowls. I tell the nurse
I feel like bolting. She says *I know it's not*
as nice as York. The ambulance man points
That's why I could never be a patient.
How do you sleep with one pillow?

Possible Outcomes

The surgeon takes out the drawer of my locker
to represent the space where he will voyage
with his endoscope. He points out
everything in this dark cave
where he will stumble with his tiny light
to cut out the cyst which is pushing up, up
against the optic nerve. To his left
my sense of smell, to his right
the mechanism that regulates peeing,
straight ahead the pulsing nerve
that gives me sight. Twice I've felt
I would black out and saw two women
on the door of the ladies, together,
holding hands, then separating.
Only once I had a patient wake up blind.

Leaflet

(found poem)

*You should avoid blowing of your nose or sneezing
for three weeks after surgery.*

*Complications: bleeding, infection including meningitis,
leakage of the fluid that bathes the brain.*

*If we do get a CSF leak, we occasionally take
a piece of fat and plug the hole.*

*Sometimes we put a drain in the spine to divert
the fluid while the hole undergoes repair.*

*There is a risk of blindness, double vision and stroke.
Any brain operation carries a risk of death.*

*The Pituitary Foundation has conducted research
which has identified several psychosocial issues:*

*increased levels of depression, anxiety,
appearance-related concerns, a reduced quality of life.*

Dee-Anna

My neighbour is wheeled back in.
I hear the handover nurse say
She's had no sleep and shouted all night.
She managed to pull out her ventilator.
I cower behind the false privacy of the curtain
which divides us. Later, she tries to ring home
but has forgotten the code to open the phone.
They ring her son and the nurse calls out 4445.
Once in the phone it's clear she's too confused
to make a call and she decides someone
has been *into it doing dodgy business.*
It must be me as I was the only person in earshot.
She wants them to call the police. I lie there,
listening to her ravings, their reassurance.
I no longer feel safe. The nurse tells me
She won't do anything, she can't even move.
Now she's shouting that they don't know
what they're bloody doing.

Consent Form

The registrar reminds me of the dangers,
scaring me all over again.
Blindness, stroke, death is the gist.
He's not anxious to proceed
on his own decision-making;
he needs the patient to do the hard part.

With the consultant it's different.
He's so young his baby's only two weeks old
and so handsome he cuts a dash on the ward round.
He weighs up the pros and cons when the posse
of students have moved on with their clip boards,
their crack-of-dawn observation of the sick.

I'm not good at decisions at the best of times
and this is not the best of times
so I say *What would you advise me*
if I was your wife? He says
You could lose your sight. I'd go ahead.
I say *Give me the pen.*

Ward Round

My head is clear. He whisks back
the curtain and sweeps on.
The room is half dark.
I lie and watch the two women
with turbans of bandages.
The registrar asks the one on the left
how she is today and if she knows
what month it is. She has to think.
2013? He says *Not the year, the month:*
January, February. The one on the right
sees the funny side. He shows her
the bright orange water jug
and she gives him the Polish word
so he gets her daughter on the phone
and she translates. *No,* she says,
she's saying the word for cup.
He takes off his glasses and hands them to her.
Okulary, she says, triumphant. He laughs,
Even I understood that. When he leaves
she's smiling but the one on the left,
who doesn't know what a month is, cries.
The nurse comes with the drugs,
asks her her name and date of birth,
whether she knows where she is.
I can't understand why I can't pick up me fork.
Outside the window, rattled by a storm,
a snowdrop cracks open the earth.

Afterwards

Make a fist for me, she says.
Now, push your heel against my hand.
Now pull my fingers towards you.

How is it I forgot this
when I remembered the words,
Do you know where you are?

She tells me it's so she can compare.
Afterwards. I had not thought,
really thought of afterwards

only of an end to the pain,
the way the ward is blurred,
the endless, endless nausea.

So matter of fact. Afterwards.
It isn't logical but I want to say
My brain is a long way from my feet.

NBM

Nothing since midnight
and the operation is at 3pm.
I'm terrified. Also starving.
So nauseous I think I will be sick.
The staff nurse gives me a pill
then an injection. The hours crawl.
I put on the gown and socks.
At 2.55 the nurse comes,
shakes her head, says *You're not going.*
I'm going to get you some food.
Sweet and sour chicken. I say
Bring me something dry and cold.
Kerrie looks worried, then laughs.
I like your style. Jennie leads me
to the nicest shower. The water is hot,
it feels wonderful. The consultant
comes, still in scrubs, apologises.
I say *I know it's not your fault.*
He isn't operating tomorrow
but a colleague could do it.
I nod, tell him I feel like a dog
thrown one meal a day.
He says *That's a bit dramatic.*

Holding Bay

Lonely as Tucker Murphy,
sole Bermudan athlete,
in the Opening Ceremony
of the Winter Olympics
which I've been parked in front of
while I wait to be operated on.
Isn't it exciting says the nurse
as the cross-country skier
dances past the cameras
in scarlet shorts.

High Dependency

The room is vast. Eight beds around the walls.
I'm by the window and can see the Humber.
Sister is with me all the time, telling me I can breathe,
talking to me, giving me drugs, making me move,
constantly refilling the beaker of water
with the lid. They have to fit a catheter after all.
The relief. I can't swallow. My whole head is filled
with cotton wool. And the pain. Sister gets me up,
I'm in a chair, they take the drip away and the mask.
My husband comes, says the first thing he asked was
Can she see? I can see. I can see the Humber.
I cry from the joy of it, the relief.
And the sun is shining. Someone is screaming.
I can feel the pain and panic. It is an animal noise.
There are no words. Next to me an old man
talks all night to dead people, calls for Ian
to bring him water. No Ian comes.
It is evening. Two policewomen are asking
the young man opposite about being attacked.
He's Polish. His account is clear. He was protecting
his little girl. I hear his words and weep in the dark
that people could do that. All day he lies still.
I get up, I can wee. I cannot stop weeing.
I have to drink water, orange, tea. They line it up.
They measure and count. I go to the toilet.
It might as well be on the moon, I'm so weak.
A physio helps me go for a walk. It takes an age
to reach the door. She says *Before you go home*
we will help you climb one step. The screaming goes on.
Ian does not come. *Water, water* the old man cries,
his mittened hands waving like a baby in a pram.
My daughter can't look at me. She says she expected worse

but she looks at the Humber a lot. At 3.30 am
they need my bed and move me back to the ward.
We are people. The Polish man is Mika,
the screamer Audrey, the old man Barry.

The Unpacking

I think at the time
the nose-unpacking
was the worst

The houseman hadn't time
to fetch the pethidine and wait
just squirted and tugged

It was lunchtime
and everyone eating
syrup sponge

After the screams
which surely came from
someone else's throat

after the begging
Oh, I can't bear it. I can't bear it
plates clattered onto trays

My neighbour was crying
on my behalf
I rang my husband

Please come Please come
I lost all pride
I put it on Facebook

longing for comfort
a child again
needing its mother

All afternoon I cried
That night the doctor came back
shook my husband's hand

said how sorry he was
he'd had to hurt me
He was so young

He was showing two students
how to do the procedure
Beforehand I joked

I'll tell you if he's rubbish
Afterwards he said
I'm sorry love I'm sorry

19

Sense of Smell

It dawns on me that everything
tastes the same but maybe
in hospital it just does.
I tell the consultant, he waves away
my worry *Let's cross one bridge at a time*
and never mentions it again.
Anyway it's not the end of the world.
We have fish and its smell
doesn't reach me. Someone brings in
KFC and to me it's odourless.
But then my nose is injured,
the bone broken, I tell myself.
Maybe when the bleeding stops.
Alastair gives me strawberries
and I think I detect the perfume.
Lydia brings forbidden hyacinths;
sensing a faint echo of that scent,
I bury my nose in their whiteness.

'The Runner'

At first I think he's a prisoner;
he's guarded round the clock.
The security man looks as if
he's losing the will to live.
It must be worse than invigilating
or keeping an eye on paintings
in some dull gallery no-one goes to.
All day he scrolls through his phone.
What goes through the patient's head
as he lies there watching
for his chance to escape?
Even a security guard needs
a comfort break. At 2 am
the intercom crackles into action
Spotted on level 3 it says,
then *He's reached the ground floor.*
Outside, the Beast from the East
howls round the hospital entrance.
I picture him, dragging his drip-stand,
dressed only in gown and slippers,
head still bandaged, heading
down Anlaby Road, past the petrol station,
Wetherspoons, the Humber,
towards the illuminated doors of The Deep.

Nobody Tells Me

It hurts more if you stand up;
in fact only last week the physio
who's practically my best friend
encouraged me to walk up and down
as far as the staircase and back
to keep my circulation going
though of course I'm still wearing
the white compression socks.
Since no-one thought to warn me
I'm up and about like a good 'un
wheeling my brain-drain stand
alongside me like it's a mate.
The nurses spot me, usher me back
to my bed, tick me off for stirring,
suggest I lie down and stay put
before I lose even more CSF.
Can't I see the level's way above
the 10 ml marker? If I get up
the headache will be terrible.
I don't point out the obvious
that the headache has been terrible
for weeks or ask why nobody
gave me instructions? I lie down
and watch the slow drip-drip
of the clear liquid and wonder
how draining it off helps the dura
to heal and what they will do
with the full bag of liquid
and whether I am losing poems
and thoughts and bits of brain
along with the fluid. Later
my husband jokes *There goes
a haiku*. I would laugh but it hurts.

Neurosurgery Ward 4 Bed 8

The drain in my spine is emptied: 10 mls
of brain fluid per hour. The nurse appears
to turn the tap. If I sit up the headache worsens

so I lie flat under my regulation cotton blanket
and, for hours, watch the pigeons dance on the rooftop
where sometimes a man appears to tie down the net.

The nurses tell me it's windy but nothing moves,
there are no trees or reeds to whisper in the wind.
How determined they are, my pigeons,

to make their nest in this inhospitable place.
It must be warm on top of the air conditioners
and behind, if the man would only let them,

they could bring twigs and mate and lay warm eggs
and preen themselves in privacy and warmth.
How I would like to preen myself. In three more days

I can shower and wash my hair. I can cut my nails.
How determined they are, my beautiful pigeons.
If only the man in grey would leave them alone.

I want to fling open the window and let in the air
and call out to them, *Thank you. Thank you*
thank you, thank you, my beautiful birds.

One Day I Started to Cry

And knew I was getting better.
It was a revelation,
like the day we buried my father
and from the funeral cortège
on the way to Scarborough Crem
I saw the rest of the world
through glass. We were passing
The Church of Jesus Christ
and the Latter Day Saints;
Jane was chatting to the vicar
about how it was the same god.
There was a little dog on the path
so excited at the smell of the sea.

To My Cyst

Flu set you going
like a ticking bomb,
growing, growing
in the cramped space
between skull and brain
which I imagine
as like a crack in a tunnel
where a buddleia
tries to flourish.
You see them from trains,
that urge to grow,
or mushrooms in a shed.
You had food and water;
you would make it.
I was your host,
me, this me that cries
and loves and is typing
these black letters
on infinite space.

Visiting Time

In here everyone talks to the dead.
Some speak aloud, Barry calls to his son;
Enid, who, after having her hip done
broke the other one getting out of bed,
talks to her late husband, telling him
This is the worst pain and I'm not joking
and I, inside my head, talk to my mum
which is ironic as we barely spoke.

I'm sorry I didn't buy you the dressed
crab that awful lunchtime. You guessed,
as I did not, it would be your last,
afterwards you'd eat little and then less
then not even sips out of a beaker,
just me wielding the sponge on a stick.

Seventy

Today I know with absolute certainty
I will not always be here.

The thought doesn't make me afraid
for today everything is beautiful;

this cake tastes like paradise,
this cold water like wine,

your face peering round the door
is the dearest face,

this poem in the book Rachel sent
is so lovely that I cry.

Even the squeak of the nurse's shoes
is comforting

even the needle I no longer mind,
even the ache in my head

for I have learnt something today.
It is good to be alive,

it is precious and I must hold it
in my hand like a bird.

Phlebotomist

He asks me my name and date of birth.
I say *11/7/1948 same week as the NHS*
and we're both on our last legs. He laughs.
I roll up my sleeve and offer him the crook
of my right elbow which is black with bruises.
I say *That's your best bet. The last time*
they put a new cannula in they had four goes.
Am I glad to see an expert. He says *No-one*
ever says that! and leaves with three phials
of blood, whisking the curtain back.
It's still half dark. Most of the day's work
is done by 9am. The ward round, the meds,
the changing of beds, the bowls of warm water.
And then it's change-over time and not
a nurse in sight. I look forward to
the day staff coming on, bright with morning,
crisp, fresh. Perhaps it will be Kerrie
with the shaved head and tattoos
telling me about getting blethered,
or Claire with the dodgy joints
or that nice student who sat with me
when I was in shock after they tugged
the dressing out of my nose.
It took me a week to suss the uniforms,
because you'd never know there was a hierarchy
and on the labels there are only first names.
I'm like the trusty in a prison now, I've been here
so long. I try not to ask for anything
because they will be running every minute
of their thirteen-hour shift and not letting on.
What I will be longing to know
is what the endocrinologist will find
in those three phials of blood

and I know if it's good news PJ,
the Charge Nurse, will come to write it
in the file and be as pleased as me.
When I told him I was writing a poem
he said he would come back and read it.
I said *Oh no, you won't!*

Saturday Night

Another long night with no sleep.
Yesterday they sent two of my room-mates home.
Sister says the ward will be full by morning,
every weekend it's the same. All the beds
will be filled with admissions from A&E,
more motor bike crashes, more patients
with medical and social needs. And on Sunday night
she'll have to ring patients with brain tumours
to tell them their operations have been cancelled.

I lie awake listening to the admissions,
the unfailing patience and kindness of nurses
and I weep. Meanwhile the sick are restless,
the young woman with the aneurysm,
the pretty girl with the tumour and the two-year-old
who cries because her mother can't come home.
It's so long till morning. The hours are endless.
I cry silently behind this blue curtain.
How long till the lights go on?

Maud

Maud is a black silhouette against
a blue curtain. Maud is my friend,
my mother, my nurse. Last week
I ran down the corridor
and wept on her; she said
I've never seen anyone so happy
just to have done a poo.
Just now she held my hand in her blue glove
while the doctor pulled the tube
out of my spine. The pain was nothing
to the agony in my head. The doctor
was kind and as quick as he could be.
He is not a father, a brother, an uncle
but he too is my friend. He cares.
He listens. He puts things right.
I need them both but it's Maud I love.

Sodium 136

A new form of torture
to raise my sodium level
which is dangerously low.
They measure out five glasses
of water into my jug
to last me till midnight,
write *1 litre fluid restriction*
on the board over my bed
so the tea trolley passes me by,
the milk-shake woman doesn't come,
the pourer of custard shakes her head.
Slowly the level creeps up.
After five days I'm fantasising
about gulping cartons of juice.
I have a tug of war with a nurse,
will not let go of the jug
which she wants to remove,
tell her if I wanted to cheat
I could put my head under the tap
and drink. I win, the jug stays.
The tea lady leaves me half a cup
and whispers *I won't tell them, love.*
I do not touch it. 117, 118,
123, 124 and then, overnight,
SODIUM 136. I weep with joy.
They rub out the notice.
I gulp down glass after ice-cold glass.

Who Knew

there is so much moisture
in a sultana, a cranberry, a raisin.
They glisten like fat, wet jewels.
I gulp the quartered pear
like a man dying of thirst.
Two juicy satsumas, segment
after segment, each bursting
on my tongue. And then
a craving for sharp apple juice
so bad that when your £2 coin
is swallowed by the machine
and the bottle still trapped,
I walk to the next ward
and beg a nurse to look
in the fridge. She places
two cold cartons in my hand.
I cannot tell you how they taste,
only the burst of moisture
in my throat. Forgive me,
Sharon. I understand
why you hid in the bathroom
with the vodka and drank and drank.
I hope they let you keep your dogs.
SODIUM 142. I'm going home.

Acknowledgements

Many thanks to the editors of the following, where some of these poems first appeared: Algebra of Owls, Magma, The North, Butcher's Dog, Coast to Coast to Coast, Poetry Space Competition Anthology 2018, The 2019 Brian Dempsey Memorial Prize Anthology, Pituitary News, Out of Context, Hippocrates Prize Anthology 2019.

The title poem, *Sodium 136*, was commended in the 2019 Hippocrates Prize for Poetry and Medicine, *Ambulance Ride* was longlisted in the 2018 National Poetry Competition, *Reading Henry James in Hospital* won second prize in the 2018 Poetry Space competition, *The Unpacking* won third prize in the 2018 Poem and a Pint competition and *Nobody Tells Me* was highly commended.

I would like to thank the endocrinology team and the staff in A&E at York Hospital and everyone in the neurosurgical department at Hull Royal Infirmary for their excellent care and exceptional kindness and also the Pituitary Foundation for invaluable support and advice.

I would also like to thank the following for their invaluable advice on the poems: Lydia Harris, Neil Rollinson, Andrew McMillan, the York Stanza, Leeds University Poetry Group, Stuart Pickford, Emma Storr, Charlotte Eichler, Ruth McIlroy and Lydia Kennaway.

A donation from every copy sold will be made to The Pituitary Foundation.